I0777187

Hypnosis and Hypnotic Gastric Band

BAGH Approach

Well being and Hypnotic Gastric Ring

Christophe Pank

Table des matières

Author of :

1/ My first steps on the Law of Attraction (Feb 2013)

2/ Journey of a Hypnosis practitioner against cancer (Fev 2015)

3/ Hypnosis and Pain Management : The study of the Hypno-Analgesia Process (Jul 2015)

4/ Limited Power : Accepting our own limits is to open up our real potential (May 2016)

5/ Hyperempiria and Self-Mastery : Apply Hyperempiria for your personal development (Jul 2017)

6 : Energetics CT (Sept 2017)

Introduction

Hypnotic (or virtual) Gastric Band is a more and more popular tool in the hypnosis and well being world. For a few years, we can find many practitioners who propose this method to all public.

We know being overweight is one of the biggest actual issues, an article from *Le Monde* (publication 10/25/16) even states that **one in two french are in excess or overweight.** It is likely that in the near future, this issue becomes one of the major causes of mortality. Without talking of death, overweight is a **real factor of suffering** for many and, without pointing at the fact that more and more fast foods are available, *many psychological elements are also to consider* in the progression of this pathology. To support and help people who wish to go back to a healthier diet, without falling into drastic diets and the famous yo-yo effect, here is one of the recognized values from the virtual gastric ring. The BAGH approach is coming from this philosophy to **bring support** and an added lever to anyone who really wants to find back a balanced diet, *in listening more justly to themselves and their needs.* The specificity of this technique **is not at all to bet on the diet aspect** (which is essential as a second step) but to find back ourselves and to realign ourselves in our relation to food, **being the most caring** possible.   I am, like many others, someone having issues with their weight since childhood. In addition, I chose to practice sport in categories which means that I always need to watch my scales, not counting that I had an illness which made me lose loads of weight.

To look on the bright side of this situation, I was able to observe from the inside **all that to be overweight meant,** all the fantasies of magical or spartan diets. Since childhood I tested hundreds of things with a constant feeling of **pressure from an external world on an inferior being** whom sooner or later was going to explode. To lose weight, to melt, to slim, to go back to your weight, whatever logic you use, there is a **sensation of duty, something that judges us constantly.** Maybe it is nutritionists, doctors, coaches, others, the world, or even forums...In all of that, I realised that *never, we were taught to listen to ourselves, to respect ourselves, to understand ourselves or just to give ourselves attention.* From these observations, I created the BAGH approach and I tested it on many partners and for free on the internet. You can find the complete program here : http://anneau-gastrique-virtuel.net. Since, I have received dozens of feedbacks, or maybe even hundreds on the **positive effects of this method.** Some have lost 10 to 20 or even 40Kg, some others 2 to 3 Kilos, but all of them tell me **how their relation with food is so much better, a stress disappeared within their relation towards eating**. Even better, many feedbacks were about the fact that even if the target of loss of weight is not quite reached, there is a *better perception of oneself and that the number is not so important anymore,* but the sensation in itself becomes then the lever to move forward at your rhythm. I don't sell dreams, as you are used to hear about miracle products or unfailing methods. The BAGH approach has good feedbacks, not for all, and **demands patience.** Patience is essential, you need to be ready to have a **24 months goals.** Yes, you read well, **two years.**

It can seem long but when you think of the number of months you had lived with your own diet, it isn't that much. This method wants to be the fairer on a **conscious, subconscious and unconscious level,** in other words by finding a mental, psychic and physical balance.

In this essay, I propose **to practitioners this approach**, so that they can adapt it according to their partners and individuals willing to lose weight, through a **logical path** to put into practice with free and available audios aswell. I want you to realise that one of the ways for a **better being in terms of weight** is to **be more caring towards yourself, more listening**. More keys which open doors that limits what pushes us to excess.

1/ What is the virtual Gastric Band ?

This technique consist in **proposing to the subconscious a real 'mental' surgery,** which projects a real surgery of having a bypass implanted. We know that even if surgeons are good, there can be postoperative risks. Most of the time, it is a refusal of the body or an infection. It is rare, but it is still scaring enough people away to not try the 'real' thing.

Hypnosis is a discipline which offers *the possibility to better communicate with subconscious* and to propose suggestions which will be lived as if real. We know that when we think of a lemon to crunch with full tooth, we are going to secrete saliva, just as if we have a lemon in our mouth. It is thanks to this **natural phenomenon,** that **everyone lives in their everyday life,** that we are going to be able to implant a hypnotic gasrtic ring. The hypnotist *proposes to his/her partner in hypnotic trance, details of the surgery so that the subconscious can validate the approach as a real one.* In other words, psyche thinks that there is a ring and most of all that **there is a need to function as if there is one.** What is particularly **reassuring** is that everything can be reversed with only one session, for example to tighten, or the opposite to release, even to take out. **There is no 'negative' physical feedback** as, for real, there has been no surgery. If some elements are awkward, you just need to talk about it to your practitioner so that he/she can **correct what is needed.**

So, the usual question for beginners : But can I be hypnotised ? There is no issue, everyone is and your operator **will find the best way for you to live your session.** What you will live will be genuinely different than what another will

2/ How to implant a hypnotic gastric Band ?

This part is specifically for practitioners, but it can be interesting for individuals who would like to understand better what they will live during their sessions.

Opposite to audios, in practices, we have the chance to **adapt our speeches** to our partners and his/her story. Feel free to add anything you want as long as it goes in the same direction as your partner. We will come back later to the **possible questionophy to take into account** before leading a ring implementation scssion. Indccd, it is paradoxically not the main goal for the BAGH approach to implement the ring, it is best to take one or more sessions to well draft the guidelines, develop objectives and work on the listening of oneself. The objective of the ring implementation is to **comfort the subconscious** in an approach and to stimulate real tapering and **behaviours towards food.** It is a **lever** more than the heart of the approach. With a ring, the partner will be less hungry, will be less in his compulsions and will succeed to eat less because the satiation becomes faster. You need to keep in mind that you will have **to suggest a situation much more than a surgery.** It is a set of steps and not only to make a few suggestions based on a mechanical process. It doesn't mean that you can't go through a Hypno-PnL approach in order to appease partners who *aren't ready to invest themselves completely* in the BAGH approach.

Once you have induced trance to your partner with either :

- A quick induction

- A relaxation induction

- An Hyperempiria induction

- A Questionosophy induction

You can orientate the first part of your work towards the **ambiance and spirit state to have.** You will allow then your partner, through your suggestions which will become deepenings, to have the right 'mindset' to optimise the motivation and the belief in the success of the implementation. Once in a **balanced trance,** you will make your partner imagine that he gets out of his/her house to go to hypnotic clinic. I insist on the idea to be the most open possible for a real will to succeed, to enjoy an exceptional day that **will change his/her life.** You can graduate his/her motivation on a scale. The way to the clinic will be a **pre-suggestion.** We enter into an awaiting phase, meaning that you will recall, step by step, to your partner that he/she is on his/her way to the clinic. The different steps are :

- Arrival and welcoming of the patient

- Night before the surgery in a luxury clinic

- Direction to the theatre

- The surgery

- The postoperative check

- The exit

We are in a suggestions stage which allow the subconscious to direct itself towards and validate with a **Yes-Set.** Once you feel that your partner is in a positive trance, you can make him arrive at the clinic. Keep in mind that some people are *phobic of medical places or simply anxious.* At the entrance, you can indicate that once in, there will be **a well being sensation,** a release from a heaviness present for many years. Make your partner penetrate the clinic and put forward the **caring staff. Caring** is the key word of the session, first to avoid pressure that sometimes patients can have for excessive quick results and then to the process. There will be moments of feeling **'down'** in the everyday life of your partner. He/she will then have to focus first on caring first for him/herself.

When welcomed at the clinic, make your partner present him/herself, *then make him/her state outloud the reason why he/she is there.* This is a direct auto-suggestion, you can make him/her repeat three times to create a pattern. Then make him/her be shown to his/her room. Put forward **smiles, agreeable environment,** other patients with positive comments, with a well-being and a joy. Insist on the serenity of the approach and the maternal staff. The room is agreeable and *the doctor is going to come to repeat to him/her the different steps since the morning after.* You start back pre-suggestions, this time more focused on the surgery and the perception. The doctor will recall that the surgery will happen the following morning and that he will make a *tiny incision* to implement the silicone ring at the top of the stomach, that he will be able to tighten it according to their needs and that the patient will be able to learn to control.

Of course, everything will **happen nicely with a hypnotic anaesthesia 100% guaranteed.** The doctor will also remind the positive effects of this procedure : Appeasement of hunger, faster sensation of satiety, loss of weight and everyday well being. You are **suggesting and already in the future.** We still have an awaiting lever and a seeding. Train your partner to the positive sleep at night. This will offer a **deepening** and a validation of the trance you opened. When waking up, play on a **deep state of relaxation** and well being with a feeling that everything is going fine. *Make him/her repeat outloud* that everything will be fine and that soon, he/she will be able to *control his/her feeding patterns with care, lose weight with balance.* Then smiling and positive nurses arrive to take him/her to the theatre. You can add some music that your partner particularly enjoys to play while going to the theatre. In the surgery room, you will let your partner lay on the table and each specialist will present himself with a smile, *with an agreeable word and a suggestion of success.* Take the opportunity to seed one more time that the session is going well, its success automatic because it is what the patient really wants. **It is important to involve him/her completely and that he/she is convinced of the potential success.** The surgery will start with a trance, which allows you to re-induce a deepening process and specify clearly, with your suggestions, that from **now on the anaesthesia is complete and deep.** You can also add an **analgesia of pains** from the past linked to food (boulimia, anorexia, compulsion...).

The surgery starts and you describe what is happening with more or less details, the idea is mainly to give **suggestions at each description** that you put in place.

The incision can be a suggestion and open to a new way of living, to see life. This way, **you do not open a body but a door towards other possibilities.** You can then spend **a little time to implant the ring,** insisting on suggestions of the everyday life. Here are some elements that you can use as suggestions and possibilities whilst implementation of the ring :

- Appease hunger in all circumstances

- Take away cravings

- Develop self control in front of sugary or salty foods

- Sculpt and slim toward the objective

- Develop caring in all situations, towards body, some behaviours

- Leave a progression notion

- To hear body alerts when satiety is reached

- To feel satiety more and more clearly

- To not compensate neither physically nor emotionally excessively

You can suggest that *the ring is in silicone* and that after a countdown, you are going to inflate it and that all *benefits are going to be in place at this moment and continue the following days.* **Involve** once again your partner so that he/she can decide that it is the moment to take responsibility for his/her choice.

You can seed regularly **expected consequences** and make the team of doctors speak as they were congratulating themselves on the **success of the integration body/spirit.** This phase confirms all the previous suggestions.

Focus now on the closure of the incision as a metaphor and continue explaining that thanks to this approach, **there will be no secondary effects, nor scar.** That this ring is special and that, with a little bit or learning, **the partner will be able to use it in order to tighten or loosen as he/she wishes.** That will allow him/her to allow him/herself with care excess, during festivals or holidays etc... You offer then the opportunity of flexibility to your partner. Once the surgery is over **you can suggest a state of well being and relaxation.** Then you can bring him/her back to his/her room to integrate the different elements. The room will be a moment where you repeat **suggestions and consequences of what you have done then, what is expected.** It is also a phase of futurisation with a possibility to check that the elements will be validated

- *Project your partner to a meal he/she is about to have when hungry.* See him/her take his/her time to chew and have the sensation of satiety arriving quickly

- Offer the possibility to **have a balanced satiety,** meaning caring to avoid all excess as anorexia

- Propose a classic method of **chewing in 21 times** to take time and avoid fattening. Once again, associate **caring,** to avoid guilt to not do it systematically

- Allow your partner to see that the meal in front of him/her is *still half full and that the desire to eat and hunger have disappeared.*

Make your partner wake up in his/her room and **do a confirmation work** (seeding) with a meal that will be brought to him/her. Suggest appeasement towards food, satiety and most of all that he/she leaves a part of the food. Note how much your partner is proud and is already in **an attitude of success** towards the ring. You can make him/her *confirm this sensation outloud.*

Make the doctor return later to **confirm all that has been put in place.** You play on the **authority value** (yours and the one projected into your session). Congratulate him/her as much as possible, insisting on the expected elements from the patient.

The conclusion of the doctor is to say that all went well and that the partner can check out as soon as he/she would like to. You can insist on **the security** of the approach and **the success** of it which will only be confirmed meal after meal, days after days. You now make your partner get out of the building and doing so, closing metaphorically a door. This allows you to make **a last point on the different suggestions** proposed. You can of course add anything according to the history of your partner. I invite you **to not go over an hour of session** for the implementation of the ring. It is enough and, as I underline often, it is not the time that we spend in the ritualisation of an approach **that will determine the success of a session.**

It happens often that ritualised trances of 5 minutes bring as much benefits as 45 minutes ones. To make it last is often a need from the practitioner.

This session is easy to put in place, but determines only one part of the BAGH approach. Keep in mind to particularly put forward the care for oneself.

3/ Caring in the Caring and Hypnotic Gastric Ring Approach

Why do I underline the importance of caring in such a mechanical technique as the ring ? We are used to, in the 'overweighted world', hearing about multiple ways *which MUST make us lose weight.* This promise automatically puts the consumer in **guilt**. The one to not succeed, the one to not look like the advertising or testimonies and results. In the BAGH approach, *we are not entering a challenge.* We are in an **awareness** of our ways and food behaviours. As said previously, I recommend to whoever listens to the audios or comes into practices to **take on a 2 or even 3 year plan to find back themselves.** This way of thinking is unique and probably not the most marketable. However, it is realistic in front of people who have been themselves overweight for years, even decades. We know that **we can't lose weight so quickly**. **Time** is an element that we value in practice, so that the notion of body changing is well understood. Except for some illnesses, *partners have taken this weight in weeks, months, years.* It is **quite a long** process, even if some heights of this can happen in some weeks. **With the system BAGH, we are not trying to cut weight** like MAIO techniques or others. I used some of these techniques myself and would fast before competitions, or for 10 to 15 days, I would then 'lose' more than 10 kilos. However, we all know, in this kind of sport, *we will regret these carbohydrate bounces and others* for years. Surprisingly, every year, magazines announce back their before-summer diet to lose 5 kilos or more in 3 weeks.

Let's be honest with our practice, we will have to learn **patience and caring** in the way our *body and psyche will work* first, how the implementation of the ring will work then...suggestions that we will make during diverse sessions.

Some people lose weight very quickly at the beginning, because the excess of weight is important, then it will take a few months for more to be lost. Some do not lose at the begining but when started, the process becomes very fluid. If nothing happens, **it is a message from subconscious explaining that the first reason for the gain of weight has not been treated** and that you need to dig into your partners life to find the real cause. So **more than the will, I insist on the care,** we are not only in an approach where the loss of weight is valued, we are in a dynamic where *we want our partner to find back his/her balance regarding his/her food behaviours.* We do not want him/her to lose 15 kilos in the next 6 months to only take them back in the 3 following years, and then having to start over. You will have to accept that *sometimes you don't lose weight, sometimes you take some back, sometimes in some circumstances it is hard.* In these moments, caring is primordial. *Don't feel guilty, criticise yourself, being angry at yourself all the time on* **your one time incapacity.** Do not go into excessive compensations. **You can learn all of this,** hypnosis by suggestions offers you a great way to program new behaviours, it will then be your choice to apply them in your everyday life and you will have **to put some fundamental work into it.** Among the best feedback I received, there is one partner who used audios, she wrote she wanted to lose 15 kilos, but that she only lost 5.

She was feeling so much better within herself that the number wasn't important anymore. With months and years, she reached the loss of 10 Kilos but most of all, she gained a new way of seeing her life, food, with extreme care towards herself. For the practitioner, you will have to make a **seeding in all sessions, to give oneself caring and time.** You will be able to **take into account the different feedbacks from body and subconscious.** Never be in failure notion. You will always have an information to use and resituate the approach of your partner. It is also important for you practitioners, to be caring towards your sessions. That is why I was saying that the implementation of the ring in itself is not the most important, it is **secondary.** At first time, you will do a **micro therapy** to resituate things. We are going to see in the next chapters some points to bring up to your partner so that he/she can be at his/her optimum state in order to get positive results. For you partners, keep in mind that it is a first step into a **24 month approach.** Make yourself a **log,** weekly or each two weeks, but more than daily. If it is daily, you are going to **become obsessed** and that is not the goal of the approach. Indeed, many other methods ask you to write down everyday your weight and what has been eaten. It **can be stressful** for many and once again, orientated towards guilt when we look at numbers and food considered 'bad'. We are caring, so on your log, write down your **monthly target**, as we are taking 24 months (or more if you would like to), you can write down a target of 1 kilo lost each month, so **possibly 24 kilos in 2 years**. I recommend again to **not go to fast** so that you do not lose motivation and keep your goals as you settled them first even if you, at the end, go faster.

In the business world we call these **'over-views',** meaning going over your goals, quite stimulating. You can also add *pictures of yourself, month after month, articles you like, clothes you want to wear in a few months.*

It is a log dedicated to bring you good so it is what needs to go inside.

4/ Work on major themes from BAGH Approach

In this chapter, we are going to look at **key elements** of the approach. I will leave to the practitioner the choice of when, according to his/her strategy of accompaniment, he/she will implement the ring. I indicated this in the start of this essay so that the interested ones in *the technical aspect can go quickly to basics.* As underlined in the previous chapter, **caring** is crucial for long term success. I am not talking of a few months of well being but of a real daily impact, **for years.** We all know that there are factors in our lives that are able to make us become overweight as compensation. In the audios, I put together a program called **Bienveillance.com**. For 28 days, the partner has 28 sessions of 5 minutes each to listen to in addition to the implementation of the ring. It is very important for me, as most of these users of *this audio program are not helped in practices and by a practitioner.*

In this section, I propose to practioners to **take into consideration** some elements which come back regularly for whoever is working on his/her weight. Of course, in practice, you have the chance to **have knowledge on the story of life** of your partner. It allows you to be much **more precise** and to **dig into** different themes that you wouldn't have with only audios. Remember that even if often we want to work on our issues, we *are very good at keeping status quo* just because it brings us **many benefits,** and the most visible is to **avoid spending energy to change our model.**

Escaping can then be redundant when we are not followed by a professional who puts us back in front of what we try to avoid.

1/ The first theme I put forward is **the internal child.** It is a classic tool of hypnosis, very useful with many practitioners. To go and **meet this token** of oneself is very intense. For many partners, it has been years that they see themselves through **a deformed image of themselves.** An image that, maybe, has followed them for decades and that, maybe, *fills them with guilt, angst, denial and other negative emotions.* Many have forgotten how they were, when they were a kid. I always start with a confirmation in my session which is that **we have been hurt during our childhood** and that you need in the first place, to go and meet yourself, and, give yourself what you didn't receive from the educational system. You will regularly have remarks like *everything went well during childhood and that the 'caretakers' were wonderful.* **It is a conscious resistance** to not work on the past. Practitioners can really take their time on this subject. In the BAGH approach, we are going to focus on the encounter of the partner with his younger self. It is not the truth, **but a perception,** which will be useful in the *appeasing process towards him/herself.* To do so it is really easy, in function of your style, you can **countdown** explaining that at the end of it the partner will meet with his younger self, *in all his/her beauty, strength but also vulnerability and expectations.* It opens the door towards a global vision of the being. Insist on the positive aspects of this child, sometimes, partners can be very hard with themselves.

In reality, this hard appearance has nothing to do with the **interior child but the interior parent** who only repeats what has been perceived through the different authority figures of childhood such as parents, teachers or coaches.

It is generally **an intense moment for partners** who don't expect some forms which take their younger self. *Maybe the child is angry, sad or feels betrayed.* It is rare that the child is joyful, for many years *no one took care of his/her sufferings and the responsible one at this stage is* **the partner.** You are not going to incriminate but on the opposite **repair.** It is a moment where the adult we have become, gives him/herself the right to forgive and to start **a new attention towards him/herself.** It is the key that we are looking for. The BAGH approach is based on this idea, **I will pay attention to myself and take care of myself.** I am not doing it for the outside world, but because **my internal world is in conflict and suffered for way too long.** It is just as if, at this moment, your partner **signs a contract with him/herself,** to give oneself everything that has not been given in the past. And this is not only through an excess of weight, food or others. In between sessions, and most of all to learn **personal discipline,** to daily meet with his/her younger self is a good way to give to the partner **the responsibility of his/her approach.** It focuses on the shared belief : it is my subconscious who does it all and if it isn't as I would like it to be, *it is not my fault.* We put conscious and subconscious aspects in the same success dynamic.

2/ The second important point to consider as with the internal child that the adult who is coming to see you, is **forgiveness.**

For some years now, we have seen the ho'oponopono approach becoming popular, an hawaïan system about forgiveness. We know that it is useful to forgive oneself. But actually, *it is not that easy to put in place.*

To do so, I use a **TPA method**. It is an **integration principle** which gives to the partner the possibility to take one step at a time, without being in a failure model which can be one of his/her **secondary patterns,** and one you want to avoid during his/her therapy. It is useful to **define what the partner needs to forgive him/herself,** either *the child towards the adult, but also this suffering adult towards him/herself, even towards the child.* There can be a need to forgive : the fact to not listen to oneselves, fears, incapacity to handle things, promises not kept, words never said...etc. As much for the practitioner as for the partner who is in this approach alone, it is useful to take a few minutes to answer honestly these questions :

- What do I have to forgive myself ?

- What do I have to forgive them ?

We are going to dig as much inside ourselves as outside, sometimes we are in a destructive model to hurt others, as some kind of indirect punishment but answering to parents, family, partner or social systems and beliefs. In other words, to not be slim and to not have a conventional job is a way to show to parents that we do not fit in and make them pay for lived constraints. We are in an approach **imposing a real sincerity on oneself.** It is useful and even more in practices, to realise things that **we are not able to forgive** ... for now.

Once we have established some elements to forgive, we are going to, **with the internal child** start to work on forgiveness. The practitioner is going to orientate suggestions in this direction. You can use the TPA this way :

- If the partner is not ready or is struggling to forgive, you can **orientate towards Tolerance** for the idea of forgiveness. It is not very involving and it is a first step towards more serenity.

- If the partner is not yet ready, make him/her do **Allow, meaning giving yourself the right to Forgive.** It could be a trigger to really forgive.

- If the partner is ready, you just need through suggestions to train him/her towards **an acceptance of forgiveness.**

A session is interactive, allowing the partner *to express difficulties, emotions and his experience with the internal child.* It can be **big emotional discharges,** even maybe a form of violence towards oneself. **Guilt is in some case so strong and anchored** for years that to change the judgment is very difficult to live. You can keep coming back in another session, if all hasn't been forgiven. You **need to respect each others timing.** It is possible to use **a tribunal as symbolic** and to orientate the partner towards a **new judgement.** You put the partner as his/her own judge, one part lawyer and the other one accused.

This way, you can identify the strong points that the partner **reproaches him/herself,** then **to defend,** and finally **to give a judgment more magnanimous,** once everything is said. It is a **dynamic refocus** on the last judgment, the last condemnation he/she imposed on him/herself years ago. It opens to a 'remission', then the freedom to give more value and care. This exercise can also **be done alone,** writing down all that *we condemn in ourselves, arguments pros and cons.* There can be a few days for deliberation, and to give oneself a judgment fairer and more caring.

3/ The third point to take into consideration is the capacity to **give love.** Many partners will **hurt themselves physically,** to punish themselves because of a lack of love for who they are. This step has to happen after forgiveness, just because it is difficult to love yourself if you are still in an excessive judgement. Moreover, caring in this approach of yourself and your attitude towards food, *can be to realise that many food compulsions are assaults and sufferings that ones gives to him/herself.* They can allow us to go over a desire which would come too fast and so instead eating a sweet or eating without stopping. The more you **give yourself love,** the more you will want to give yourself love. Indeed, it is rare that we want people that we love to suffer, *we put in place strategies for them to not be hurt or hurt themselves.* Love is an **excellent motor to protect** and in this case, from ourselves. **Love becomes a protection** towards violence on ourselves that we put in place for years.

We can use the two precedent elements to **continue seeding** and put forward our capacity to accept this internal child, to forgive him/her, and to oneself. It will automatically generate more caring and love for oneself. For some, it is not easy, in this case, *make him/her define what is, at this moment of the session, representing love.* The possibility to define the concept allows one to fully understand the measure of the words and suggest them, so that he/she can integrate the notion. In other words, *we fragment perception and step by step propose it to the partner by suggestions.* **It is easier to digest and so more realistic.** Be conscious that to say or suggest in hypnosis : love yourself, isn't sufficient. It can indeed echo and have diverse influences according to their history. This is the reason why it is needed to well define the term so that it can fit better. It can also happen that some partners assimilate love with too many difficult things, in this case, **change semantic.** You can first talk about **caring, welcoming or self respect.**

This part allows our partner to work on one of **his/her resources.** He/she will be able to create **an anchor,** thanks to your accompaniment, **on the notion of love as a protective area.** To give oneself love is to protect onself from excess. It is also to have the possibility to see food in a different way. **To be balanced** and not to enter into excessive diets and yet again violent to oneself. It is to accept to eat less sweets and to substitute them with fruits, less meals heavy in sauce and more greens. *To do so lovingly, meaning in respect of your desires.* If your partner eats 5 chocolate bars a day, would you suggest him/her that it is 'bad' and impose him to stop? First, it is removing responsibilities and second, it is violent.

It is better to suggest **to diminish slowly** food less healthy, for the ones which are better for the approach. If during the months of the programme, he/she is at one bar per day or each two days, he/she will still have his/her pleasure while feeling in control of him/herself. He/she will be caring towards his/her own progression.

4/ **Put forward to manage rather than to control.** It is an element which can be treated during a few sessions, even maybe therapy. We are in a world where anxiety pressures are multiples and can easily saturate many personalities. *The common solution is to control.* Control can be on oneself but, most of the time, it is very prevalent onto the surrounding world, *and then controllers become controlled by a system which they can't get out of anymore.*

In the BAGH approach, **the idea is to allow the partner to find back some freedom in his/her relationship to his/her body and in doing so, to food.** The excess of food control needs to not make them **dependent upon a model** that they will feel guilty if not followed. We can clearly see this in protein-rich diets, once over, users are feeling guilty to not eat 'as before'. We can even see it more in other practices like 'fasting', where users are feeling guilt over not fasting their 16hours or to have fed after the time limit. Discipline should'nt become a cell, it shouldn't confine. *Control is to not buy this packet of salty nuts so that you don't plunge in it, to not start.* **Managing is to open the packet, take a nut and to leave the packet in front without having to take more.** Managing is a flexible approach, it is an appeasing way. Control is way more rigid and puts us into tension.

I am a specialist of control and rigour, which made me **take a huge amount of weight** following **months of control, even years.** That we use control as a lever towards managing is coherent, **that we become slave of control and so of non-control though,** is less caring. You probably do not want to lose weight to gain it back right after, you do not want to control yourself for months, so that when the goal is reached, you have still **to control yourself and maintain until the end of your life.** Creating tensions bigger and bigger physically and psychologically, with the risk to go into overcompensation and to plunge into a **non-control** more and more frequent, and in doing so, to gain more weight. The idea of the BAGH approach is to allow yourself, through the work you operate on yourself, **to avoid to stay in control and to learn to manage.** The hypnotic gastric ring has the advantage to give new sensations towards food. There is less hunger, less snacks and more balanced quantities. It allows to indulge oneself in the timing of the feeds, on quantities and step by step on the products. When we manage, we know that **we can decide** to spend festivities to eat like an ogre...and without guilt. It is a choice, it is a desire and so it doesn't provoke **stress.** Moreover, in this 'managing' notion, we are trying to give back to our partner a return to freedom. One of the elements which prevents the majority **is the scale.** For many, the number becomes an obsession, each day, *partners weigh themselves on the scale waiting for a result, a change, but of course a reduction.* An advice that I give to all who start the BAGH approach, is to put the scales in a closet and to only take it out **once a month.** Why a monthly weighing ? Simply because *we have monthly goals.*

So why being bothered by numbers which can vary each day. *We want to work in depth and not on the form.* For practitioners, you need to seed this information and during one of the trances, maybe during even the implementation of the ring, you can insist on this notion to not weigh. I invite the partner to find a **'witness clothe'.** It is way more encouraging than weighing. There are some curious things in body changes. We can not lose, even gain when we have changed our life mode and feeding habits. Simply because *we take on muscles, which are heavier than fat.* However, **silhouette can change, we can get thinner and see our physique change.** We try step by step to manage the image that we have of ourselves. It is possible that partners may be for years, and without knowing it, suffering from **body dysmorphobic disorder**. In other words, they can't see themselves but through a difformed filter. Which is our next point.

5/ To work on **diforming filters**. We can teach our partners to **manage submodalities.** It is a way to refocus and teach between the practitioner and the partner. If we see ourselves in a certain way, it is because we put on filters which don't correspond. Sometimes it is the outside world who **imposed** this vision onto us. Is the thin waist more 'attractive' than a larger one ? Is the muscled body more manly than a little belly? **Obsession and the activation of negative anchors** can orientate our partners to despise themselves and once again to punish themselves for not being 'as they should'. It feeds a destructive pattern and prevents from seeing oneself in an unbiased way. This step is crucial, it leads **towards a capacity to be satisfied in ourself,** of what is put in place, to see ourselves with more and more **care on a daily basis.**

First, **we offer a work on the ideal self,** which often is a wrong image of ourselves that, even if we get close, is never reachable. You probably notice that the most 'beautiful' people for you, still **find a way to not be loving towards themselves** and will even criticise details that you didn't even notice. It is important to not be confused between **a level of requirement and a fantasy,** which reactivate a daily violence. Go and have a chat with bodybuilders, you will see that even they who exacerbate a work on their body, always find them 'not enough' or not how they would like to be. We are opening **the door to more tolerance, care and welcoming** what the partner is and will be. To do so, do not hesitate to interrogate classical points of coaching :

- When will you be satisfied of this approach ?

- What would make you happy to observe while working through this approach ?

- If you can't reach the ideal image of yourself, will you be able to accept who you are ?

- What can you accept of yourself and of your body during your implication ?

Always build **a link with the approach.** Remember, we have **24 months,** it is a time which will allow us to really put in place **new patterns**, to test them, to correct them also if needed. We are not in a research of result, which can be only an ideal, **but a way to be involved** in the approach, a real focus on what is going to be put in place, accepted or refused.

In weight coaching, we have taken the habit to ask partners to take a **picture of the ideal** they would like to reach. I have been nicely surprised by many people, who want to follow a stable approach, **using a plus sized model, far away from social ideals.** When you ask your partner to come with a **goal-picture** of the body he/she expects, do not hesitate to *point out to them excessive pictures, too slim, even skinny and always take into consideration the notion of realistic goals.* Do not hesitate to also ask for pictures for the transitions during the loss of weight. It gives **a possible satisfaction at each step of the way.** Daily the partner can take time to debrief in order to give oneself care and to see him/herself through filters. Take more and more **satisfaction** to what is put in place. Keep in mind that it is also a step in managing.

6/ In this approach of self image and deformed filters, you also need *to take into consideration the social environment* and the impact that this will have on the process, put in place by the partner. Many overweight individuals have developed *erasure strategies or more rarely of compensation by putting themselves forward.* During the BAGH approach, you need to take into consideration that these strategies can **resist or explode.** We need to understand here that the **looks of others are interpreted** by all, but even more by overweight individuals. To give you an example, just picture the last time you had an imperfection on your face (a spot, scar, bruise), how you felt everybody saw it. This is what most overweight individuals live daily. It is a **deformed reality,** most of the time, people don't care about others and how they look.

The issue is that partners will be so sure of this reality that *they are ready to put in place patterns to suggest this idea or this critical mind of others.* This is why the previous step is so important in this approach. We are going to help the partner to **be conscious of the consequences of the physical transformation** and allowing him/her to **educate him/herself** with a new self perception. A focus is needed, on the attention from others which **could grow.** For example, an overweight woman avoiding men's eyes by getting slimmer and as her figure changes will maybe *generate desire from men who so far didn't show interest.* It is important to put your partner in situation. Do not think that for men, it would be more comfortable, most wouldn't have lived this situation or didn't realise that they had seduction power. Looks and expressed desire from outside will have to **be handled, accepted and sometimes resituated.** Also, it is important that there is no *excessive compensation,* by objecting future encounters. It can also **make the environment of your partner more difficult.** Let's go back to the example of the previous woman. She is married and since she started, she modified some of her behaviours, she will **say no** to some invitations to restaurants or others. She is losing weight and her husband starts to be more and more **agressive.** At first, he doesn't say anything as **his wife feels better and better,** but when she starts to feel more confident and care for her body, she starts to buy less ample clothes, more fitting. It can create a **jealousy** from the husband who isn't used to have his spouse taking as much care of herself. Maybe, he even chose his spouse with more weight, *for himself to feel more secure, regarding his own figure and the ones of others.*

Progressively, he would maybe change his attitude and *become angry* to his wife for her changes. We know that the looks of others are impacting a lot. It is rare to realise that *even the looks of our closest ones can hurt as much.* It can even sabotage the whole approach.

We are going to propose a few strategies to manage others and their looks. Once again submodalities and even Swish Patterns can allow to not ' suffer' looks and keep them neutral.

5/ The most current questions

Since I proposed the BAGH approach and the Gastric ring, I had the chance to exchange with hundreds, maybe a good thousand of people, who wanted to test it. There are questions which always come back in practices or at home. In this chapter, I propose a kind of **FAQ section** to allow yourself to understand the whole process which is so much more than just the loss of weight.

1/ Will the hypnotic gastric ring help me to lose weight quickly ?

We are in an approach **which takes time.** It is a fact to take into consideration, the practitioner is here to **accompany you long term,** even if you are going to see him/her only a few times during the two years. As I indicated before **we are planning on 24 months,** it is most of all a **rehabilitation approach,** *physical but also psycho emotional.* It took years, decades, to get to this weight. ***Excessive expectations should be pointed out during a pretalk and the presentation of the method.*** Sometimes, the overweight is so important that **you will get thinner very quickly at first.** It is important *to not take this quick loss as a reference for the rest of the following months.* It is important to clarify that so that there is no disappointment **which may sabotage the work. Time** is an element that we can demonstrate on the *metaphoric principle of the tree.*

You will just need to *give the image of the seed which will take its time to grow and even if, at first, the changes happen fast, in years, the growth is less visible.*

Does that mean that the tree stopped growing ? No. But time confirms roots and the state.

As practitioner, you decide to put in place a BAGH follow up (or another similar you create), I can invite you to put in place sessions of **focus, questionophy, work on causes, then once each trimester a follow up.** This meeting allows you to continue to work on new emerged elements : stress, situations, psychic tensions... Possibly, you will tighten or loosen the ring, you will have feedbacks to help to adapt what is needed. In conclusion, do not sell fast results, even if they are possible, the effort will have to be continued even if there is a stabilisation or a gain of weight. It is minimum 2 years.

2/ I put on weight since I started the BAGH approach, what should I do ?

It is a question asked oftenly by the audio users. In practice, it will be **more rare.** Mostly because in practice you spend some time **to work on the history of your partners.** It allows you to understand the dynamic and strategies put in place in this gain of weight. **It isn't a monologue.** Hypnosis isn't **a spirit dictature.** Trance opens a hyper-suggestability but *isn't imposing things unilaterally.* **Subconscious gives informations in return** and when the conscious of the partner can't translate the message, it is reorientated through the unconscious, meaning the body. It is something to take into consideration as much for the practitioner as the partner, it is possible that suggestions for the ring or appeasement regarding foods *had awakened a fear, a souvenir, recalled a traumatic event, that the partner wouldn't have dealt with yet.* The body becomes then the message.

The gain **of weight is here not as 'an issue' but a message.** This message can't be translated biologically as we are used to. Why ? Simply because then, we are still not respecting the subconscious communication. Once again, we would **impose** a validated message from the conscious but **not in relation with the subconscious.** To make it simple, if sometimes **it takes a bit more time,** do apply **questionophy.** It will help you in discovering elements of comprehension. If the partner comes back to the practice **with a gain in weight**, there can be many reasons to explore. First, **is it a numerical gain ?** Meaning that the scale would indicate the gain...or is it a real marked physical change ? On the adipose tissues, fat mass increased...etc. As we saw before, *it is possible that the gain of weight is due to a gain in muscle.* If in your approach, you encourage to start a physical activity, *the muscle mass will increase and weigh more.* **Think of the clothes references.** It is a way to avoid this kind of issue. Another important point would be to look at the drinks, especially alcohol. Many people who have **alcohol issues** will have trouble to lose weight. Any kind of alcoholism (social, festive, moderate or others) will have to be sorted before the issue of weight. **There are priorities in pathologies.** Often, by working on difficulties linked to alcohol, consequences could be seen in weight issues. *It is possible to have surprising snowball effects as many things are all intricately linked together.*

Knowing that **the weight is a message,** being followed by a practitioner or using this approach at home, there are questions to take into consideration :

- How did I feel when I started ?

- What happened in my life these last weeks, these last months ?

- In my environment, were there changes ? Work, family, friends, sport ?

- Did I feel anything particular since the implementation of the ring ? Pressure/anxiety/Images... It could give information on what is happening in subconscious and indications on the message.

If you are using this approach at home, it is maybe the moment **to go and see a practitioner,** to work on causes and messages. If you are going to a practice, then this is an indication that something will need to be treated and has not been yet indentified.

3/ I sometimes have cravings or compulsions, is it normal ?

Work on compulsions and addictions, like sugar or specific foods **is to be made separate.** It is, of course, useful to be aware of this since the first sessions so that we can **seed,** session after session and in the **conversational process.** However, it is not the heart of the first sessions which should be more dedicated to clear goals, focus/refocus and the ring implementation. It is interesting to note that compulsions often have diminished, though it is still annoying to see them come back. We know that, when something difficult disappears and comes back later...it will only be stronger. At first, **I invite partners to give up.** It may seem weird but we are in a caring approach.

It is not useful to go towards frustration. Obviously, **between the sporadic craving and the daily one,** there is a delta. It stays rare that the craving is daily oppressive. If your partner tells you this, do not hesitate to dedicate one whole session on the matter. To accept to listen to the craving, can show that the dependance in itself doesn't have such an important place anymore. It is a natural and agreeable refocus. There is also a possible work which can be done, it is a bit more difficult : **alarm need/desire.** To put it in place on specific occasions can be a powerful lever to reposition and develop your **self management.**

At first, you can work on the **awareness** of what is a desire and a need. In other words, **to remind yourself of the basic signals** of our body/spirit/emotion so that it is understood, and accepted. Remember that we slowly but surely **closed ourselves from our internal communication.** Not about everything but certainly on that subject of food, *the conscious didn't succeed to understand the direction of the subconscious, meaning that the latest had to communicate with the body instead.* We are in a classic dynamic of transmitter and receiver. You can , as practitioner, use this image : the cellphone ones or any network and explain that everything need to be 'online'. By working in being conscious back on our desire and needs, our partner can **go over these few seconds that lead him/her to his/her compulsion.** The need is an element linked to a **physiologic lack which should make one feel hungry.** However, the information 'hunger' is often put aside and has been assimilitated as a lack, not only linked to a physical state. Most overweighted partners have associated *hunger to a psycho- emotional state, the body here being 'an option'.*

By feeding the body of food, you appease your mental and emotions. *It puts to sleep the psycho-emotional ackwardness by a biological link :* **digestion.** We use energy to digest and as a consequence the spirit is calmed down and so emotions. In the hypnotic approach, we can offer this idea to our partner and make him/her go back to a moment where he/she was really hungry. It will be easy, most of overweighted people had tried many diets, have spent days to fast or to diminish their level of feeding, until being very hungry. **To reactivate this anchor is something that we will be able to use to associate it to the formulation of a need.** It is an essential point which will allow to better listen to oneself, to be more aware when we give into a desire and not a need. When this refocus is done, even without an hypnotic suggestion, it opens new potential levels of awareness. *The strength of the practitioner will be to well implement this anchor and the recognition of the signal, to get back this ability to choose the attitude to have whether it is a desire or a need to eat.*

In our caring approach, the possibility to accept to have a desire and to give into it, will offer him/her a victory in his/her personal approach.

4/ Is it normal that I loose less weight than my friend who have done the same approach ?

Without noticing, **the external world has taken over more and more space in our lives.** In the overweight scenario, it is frequent that we let ourselves *be influenced still by advertisment and magical promises.* The most difficult is to **take out the competition spirit** that we put in place in this approach.

Most of the time, coaches will explain that you need to be motivated and try to go beyond oneself. It is an interesting dynamic, but when it comes to weight, all chances are that your partner will already have tried the 'go beyond yourself' strategy and that the results of this is that he/she is in consultation for the ring or listen to the audio mp3. It proves that **it is not a universal path,** and even more, that for many people, it is a spirit state that doesn't work for them. If the implementation has been done around the same time than a friend and the **competition/go beyond oneself spirit** shows itself again. I can see it also into the many online forums on which different speakers, **share their success and hindrances,** influence positively and also negatively others speakers. For example : someone loses more than 8 kilos and half, he shares pictures and his success, to motivate others. However for others, during that same period of time, they only lost a few hundred grams. It creates a comparison, and one that can be hard on the mindset. It is because, **we do not considere our uniqueness.** It is a very frequent paradoxe in therapy. *Everyone wants to feel different, even can claim it, but when things don't happen 'like for others', we do not accept our specificities anymore.* It is useful to allow our partner to refocus on the caring and that, sometimes, the beginning takes more time. The author of **Gabriel Method** explains that for him, it is the start that is the most difficult and that once body and spirit are in sync with one approach, **things become natural.** For practitioners, this way of thinking is great for two reasons :

- **Substitution** through visualisation. It can be an added lever for your partners and refocus their beliefs.

- **A change of paradigm,** too often accepted and maybe even self realised. We think that the first kilos are the easiest to lose and that after it will be difficult. It is often the case, but not always.

We will have to take our time to allow our partner to reconsiderate things and especially **to diminish their comparison spirit.** Take a moment to offer an awareness of **his/her unique way to receive suggestions** and maybe to also see what can be still in the way of any added amelioration.

5/ I don't have anything to do except coming to the sessions / Listen to the audios ? All will happen on its own with the BAGH approach ?

It is an answer that you, practitioners, can easily answer, especially in a **good pretalk.** Hypnosis, and the BAGH approach is no exception, are not **magical.** The first step is of course to **follow suggestions and to live them the more intensely possible**, to share what happens within you during the session. A practitioner can easily modify some suggestions so that they are more precise and more positive for the partner. It is important to **play your role as partner** and to be the most active possible during sessions, sharing everything happening within such as the emotions or sensations felt. In the case of audios, partner can't necessarly share what he/she lives but he/she **can stay the most active possible in his/her approach,** plunging as much as possible into his/her conscious with the different audios. I had a recurrent feedback on the audios : the sensation of falling asleep. **It is an escape.**

We all have our psychological strategies of **avoidances (or escapes)** regarding our difficulties. Paradoxically, *even if our mental seems to really want to move on or change,* maybe, it is not really the case, there are many different logics possibles.

A/ Either we lie to ourselves in **an idealised self** and we have to work on it. There is too much of a difference between expectations and the reality lived. The work on the weight will not be an approach *permitting to lose it but a call to the subconscious to work on another point 'considered' more important.* It is **another signal** which we discussed previously. This time, **the body is the messenger to go towards a deeper issue.** These are elements to considere, simply because the first motivation will not at all be the issue to solve. The partner must be **ready and active** in the approach, even **if the symptom is not dealt with right away.** It will be particularly **frustrating.** *To start an approach in which you want to obtain a result, here to lose weight and to find oneself to deal with emotions and past memories, it can be not the most pleasing.*

It is where the partners role is important, in his/her ability to **reorientate** his/her approach. Let's be honest, most of the time, the partner will think that the **practitioner is incompetent** and that the approach doesn't work, **he/she will quickly stop** (even the audios).

B/ Or we put ourselves in passive mode. Meaning that we decide to do something but our subconscious, going towards the success of what is asked, *realise that the effort to succeed will be big in modifications and to find back a balance psycho-physical.*

At that moment, the partner might block, possibly with drawsinesses to **not integrate suggestions** made by the practitioner or the audios. I know that lots of people in the hypnosis world consider *that during sleep we are in a receiving mode,* I do not adhere to this school. However, I find the information to put to sleep interesting to exploit and **to discover what is avoided.** In the work on the symptom weight, during the different theme that the practitioner will approach, there will be **emergences which the partner will be more or less conscient.** In practices, our exchanges with the partners allow us to well underline these key points. Sometimes, the emotion or sensation is very hard to translate, which can be long. If we succeed to put in place this exchange, there will be **possibly resistances,** with forgetfulness or emotional excess which will **put a distance with the information.** It is a realisation which can only be made with a practitioner. It is often for this reason that I invite users who work with audios, to go and see a professional. **It is a limit of the approach by distance.** We know that our avoidances are **effective strategies.** It is important that we realise that **our subconscious doesn't protect us all the time.** It is a point of view that many practitioners will share. A few years ago while studying Gerald Kein, I learnt that he liked to say that in the subconscious **'there is laziness'.** And it is what regularly happens, **the subconscious do not like to destroy its balance,** because there will be work to do. *Sometimes, even small elements that we realise forces us to modify some patterns and...we don't like it. Even if the new model is a positive potential.*

Between living a situation that we know, even if ackward, and having to adapt to a better 'potential', we choose to spend the less energy until we have no more choice.

Another point to take in consideration and to share with our partners, is the work in full conscisouness. It is quite fashionable at the moment. To do so, I invite you to work with the **Hyperempiria approach.** When your partner will be hungry or when he/she will be eating, it is useful to make him/her develop a trance of full consciousness. Here is a very simple method, **Don Gibbons'.** You can do it during a session and anchor it with a **classic mudra such as forefinger-thumb or thumb-middle finger.** Hyperempiria is an **ascending trance,** so, at first, make your partner realise when he/she has his/her eyes open, of all the elements present in the room. As **the peripheral sight** is more an more important, start to make him/her aware of his/her hearing, all the sounds such as your voice, breathing, external noises...here again, we develop a **peripheral audition** which will be associate to the sight. Really take the time to live this experience and do not hesitate to ask to your partner a confirmation of his/her feelings about it. Keep going with physical sensations, maybe where the partner is seated, sensations of his/her body, the heat or freshness, tensions or relaxations etc... You are going to do a **peripheral kinesthesia.** Think that the body will be able to open opportunities **for taste.** This will multiply the attention given towards chosen and eaten food. Once your partner is in an awake state and, of course, this sensation **is agreeable enough,** take a time to anchor this sensation. Once full conscisousness is here, it is easy to use. To do so, you need to make things 'emerge' and to test.

You are going to work on basic suggestions such as :

- Each time you are hungry, **you will put yourself in full consciousness** and check if you are in desire or need mode.

- Each time you choose to eat, you will take the time to **be aware of** tastes, textures, sensations but also the nutritive aspect for your body.

- Regularly I add a mastication principle such as : each time that you put food into your mouth, **you will chew 21 times before swallowing** in order to be fully aware of what you are doing and doing so, to care in your way of feeding yourself.

- Each time you eat, you will **particularly pay attention to what you smell, feel, see, perceive with pleasure.**

- When you start a meal, you will do your **mudra** in order to automatically enter into this hyperempiria capacity.

Of course you can add what you want and depending of the story of your partner. This awareness offers the possibility to live less compulsions and most of all **to focus on what the partner desire.** This approach to go towards the full consciousness is one of the daily tasks that the partner will have to put in place. So, here it is, a concrete action and the practitioner will, with each feedbacks given on difficulties or moments lived without conscious, underline indications of dissonant trances intervening in desires to eat.

6/ Do I have to have a diet besides ? What do I need to eat ?

We are not nutritionists, we need to stay where our competencies are. Invite your partner to go and see a specialist on the subject. As I proposed earlier in this essay, *I focus on finding back an appropriate feeding for the partner, listening better to oneself needs, respecting also desires and managing yourself.* We saw that **caring and the full consciousness** will accompany the path of the partner through the BAGH approach. You must also **be coherent** and avoid to eat all the time rich food or too oily or too sugary. Normally, you are going to be more close to yourself and you are going to put in place **new desires and needs,** more adequate for you and more naturally : fruits/vegetables will be part of your daily feeding. In order to lose weight, I advise to find yourself back justly and carefully, with your feeding but also to do some physical activity. Two days ago I was reading again and from a body builder that to have his appearing abdominals, everyone thinks he works at the gym...when really for him, it is **30% at the gym and 70% of adequate feeding.** I found this comment quite relevant on the fact that it is important to change our way to feed ourselves in **the most healthy way** for us. *Avoid compulsions, remember that it can create stress which increase the gripp of hunger and potentials increase of weight.* Sport is a non-negligible element. When I talk about physical activity, I am not talking about footing or going to the gym. It is important to **find back a dynamic of action.** An overweight body is much more difficult to use and often, in hasty resolutions, partners can decide to invest in special tools, subscriptions or even coachings. It is good but **often too violent.**

It is crucial to not let yourself once again go for an **idealised self**, you can work this with a practitioner. I practice sport almost daily since 25 years, since my sickness, I took 20 kilos even if I still practice a lot. **Sport is not the ultime key.** *But, to train with a little too much kilos is tiring, it is difficult for the heart and muscles. Moreover, there are tendons which could really suffer from exercice, so be careful.* An overweighted individual, once again, **have to be caring** with him/herself and **move forward step by step.** The first thing to put in place, or to offer, is to go for walks or similar. Swimming, Qiqong or some Yoga practices can do aswell. *All depends where you are at in your excess of weight.* It is much more useful to train a little regularly than rarely and excessively. You can , at first, start with a walk of 10 minutes daily or 3 times a week...then, once you see your body can take it, increase the time to 15-20 minutes. It may look not so much, but it is more respectful than to plan for 15-20 minutes footing once a week which will be so hard on your body that you will discard it very quickly.

Once again, time is important to take into consideration. Also, with the loss of weight to expect, to move will be more pleasant and you will find back a new dynamism. So, **to practice sport without hurts** to increase quantity step by step and through the BAGH approach.

Be caring with yourself and avoid competition with others.

7/ Does the Hypnotic Gastric Ring has side effects ?

One of the advantage of the ring is that, from a physical point of view, **there is no postoperative traumatism.**

It is something to notice. There is no fear to have negative feedbacks when the ring is implemented. You will probably have people contacting you because they *feel nauseous after the session.* It happens for a few reasons, the first, as we saw before, the ability to self-sabotage and resistance. In this case, *it is probably that we didn't work on a part of the story of the partner.* This is for this reason that I prefer to work first in deep with the partner. The second, the **excessive expectation** put in place by the partner and the **fear** of the session, in addition to **beliefs** which have not been released. It is sometimes a mistake on our part, as practitioner, we didn't take enough **time** to explain correctly the approach. It is also possible that our partner has eaten just as normal. During the implementation of the ring, you suggested that hunger will diminish, but the alarm is not well heard just yet, we can talk about **beta-tests.** I saw for myself **imposing mistakes.** To impose, in my understanding, is when we impose a suggestion to oneself, that subconscious give a feedback, but that we don't respect it. When I say that it is useful to work on different aspects before the implementation of the ring, I do so because I observe it first hand on myself. Following my illness and my big gain of weight, I tested many times the ring on myself, in different ways. I tested the opposite way to what I propose in the BAGH approach, which was *quite violent for my body and spirit* . By forcing, my subconscious was telling me to work on something else, to be more patient. I was working everyday on the subject and I installed it for weeks, then I started to **have abdominal pain and stronger and stronger compulsions.** That is when I decided to listen better to myself.

This was implying that I needed to stop worrying about my weight and work on deeper issues. It is important to be aware of this as much as user as practitioner. I realised at this moment that **the only symptomatic work can not have only positive feedbacks,** or even more to cut ourselves from important things.

Of course, during this time, you have to accept what is bothering you and stay focus on the essential things. My advice is *to avoid imposing and to go dig where there are traumas or other dissonant patterns.*

8/ I had a Bypass, can I still use the BAGH system ?

It is a very common question as some people after the Bypass surgery do not experience the results expected and want to try something else. I invite them first **to ask to their doctor.** Even if there is 'no danger' in reality, it is always important that there is a **medical follow up.** If there is no counter-indication, you can then implement the ring. I would strongly recommend that you first try *to figure out with the body why there was a denial of the physical ring.*

To do so, you have a few possibilities, I invite you to use **questionophy.** Put your partner in trance and ask questions, you will have informations. It can be a **whole session.** Of course, there is every chance that your partner isn't open to your questions. The hypnotic ring being only the 'ultimate' solution in a magical kind of thinking that you will have to point out in pretalk. The other way is interesting but not necessarly working. It is the **pretest therapy principle**. We are going to put our partner in trance and with pretests start to ask questions.

It is the same principle than signaling, this is why I am not 100% confident. It can be part of the **questionophy phase** when ritualised. It will give positionings and possible orientations to take into account.You can check if really the partner is ready to put everything in place for his/her loss of weight...and you might be surprised but most of all, the partner will be able to grind some teeth.

9/ A partner doesn't seem overweight, should I still do a BAGH approach ?

This question is really for practitioner who can receive partners who have a complete distorted image of themselves. We have to question ourselves to know if the loss of weight could not *become an issue, even nourrish eating disorders.* If the person is anorexic or boulimic, we can't play his/her game. In this case, I invite you to work in therapies or refocus during questionophy. As a reminder by the way, always think to inquire if there is no eating disorder : The work on these disorders is quite complex and it is useful to know if there has been a **medical transit.** In this case, and especially with eating disorders, do not work on the ring but instead, propose a complete therapy **in accordance with his/her doctor.**

10/ Can I implement a gastric ring if I am pregnant ?

Many women try to not take too much weight during their pregnancy. The first time I was asked this, I was rather surprised. I invite you to **be caring towards yourself and your body.** The body changes during the pregnancy, it can be the subject of a work through in trance with submodalities and futurisation, to help integrating the idea.

I also had the case of a woman starting the ring without knowing that she was pregnant. She didn't had any specific issues, she talked to her doctor who didn't see any inconvenient. **Do not hesitate to talk to your doctor.**

If gaining weight is a real issue at such as a moment than pregnancy, there is probably some other things to look into.

11/ I didn't lose much weight but I feel better, do I have to keep going ?

Most of the time, when you receive your partner, you work with him/her to go towards his/her goals, ones that will be **Precise – Realistic – Ecological and measurables.** It is quite normal to organize a time during sessions to check if everything goes well and is as positive possible in order to continue the personal work. Your partner may feel **a better being, even a well being.** It happens that with a few less kilos and sometimes far away from their goals, there is **a real relief, a wish to stop there.**

Don't push, it is much more positive to let the well being work on your partner. And what is amazing is that the body **will continue to regulate itself.**

6/ Conclusion

In this essay, I presented the key concepts of the BAGH approach. The most important one being : **caring.** This concept is to be assimilated to move away from the simple technique. To be overweighted is an issue that not only have an effect on the body, **but also on the spirit.** There is a lot of dislike for overweighted people. Even the word 'overweighted' show the internal struggle. It is just like if all thoughts, *cognitives schemes always nourrish a closed system which leads to an overload.* The caring work and the hypnotic gastric ring allows **the scheme to be open**. As a switch, offering to be more respectful towards yourself and your body.

Of course, it is not **THE miracle approach,** it does ask a real investment. There is a work on oneself to put in place, you will have to be ready to work on yourself for **2 or 3 years.** However, results are real and especially long term. An awareness of yourself, of who we are and what we want. A better management of yourself on feedings but also different other aspects of life. Everything is linked in our psyche, this approach offers a way to be unified within and to respect yourself.

Take care of yourself,

Be One

Pank (16 janvier 2017)

Who is Christophe Pank ?

I am French and live in Paris. I have worked in hypnosis, NPL, personal development and energetic healing for more than a decade. Everyday, I share my experience and knowledge. To optimise my work, I created HnO (Hype-N-Ose) Hypnose in 2010. As psycho-practitioner, I can help people to learn about themselves, to increase their knowledge.

I am now sharing my ideas in essays, videos and audios. The more you open your mind to different ways of thinking, the more you develop your capacity to become who you really are.

Take the time to watch my english Youtube Channel : hnohypnosis and my website : www.hnohypnosis.com